Hey Kids! Let's Visit Dublin Ireland

Fun, Facts, and Amazing Discoveries for Kids

Teresa Mills

Life Experiences Publishing

Copyright © 2024 by Teresa Mills

All rights reserved.

No portion of this book may be reproduced in any form without written permission from the publisher or author, except as permitted by U.S. copyright law.

Contents

Welcome	1
A Little About Dublin	3
1. Temple Bar	9
2. Trinity College	13
3. Dublinia Viking Museum	17
4. Dublin Castle	19
5. National Museum of Ireland	23
6. St Stephen's Green	29
7. Little Museum of Dublin	33
8. Saint Patrick's Cathedral	35
9. Merrion Square	37
10. Dublin Mountains	41
11. Ha'Penny Bridge	45
12. The Jeanie Johnston - Irish Famine Story	49
13. EPIC Irish Emigration Museum	53
14. National Leprechaun Museum	57

15.	National Botanic Gardens	61
16.	14 Henrietta Street	65
17.	Phoenix Park	69
18.	Dublin Zoo	73
19.	Dún Laoghaire Harbor	77
20.	Dublin Tours	81

Welcome

Dublin is the capital city as well as the largest city in Ireland. It is full of history and exciting things to see and do. In Dublin, you can explore castles like Dublin Castle and learn about Dublin's past at the National Museum of Ireland. Dublin is a city full of history and charm, ready to be explored!

This book is written as a fun fact guide about some attractions and sites in Dublin. It includes some history interspersed with fun facts about things to do. The book can easily be enjoyed by younger children through reading it with them. You can visit Dublin right from your own home! Whether you are preparing for a vacation with the family or just want to learn a little more about Dublin, Ireland, this book is for you.

As you continue to learn more about Dublin and Ireland, I have some fun activity and coloring pages that you can download and print at:

https://kid-friendly-family-vacations.com/dublinfun

When you have completed this book, I invite you to enjoy the other books in the series. We visit Washington DC, a Cruise Ship, New York City, London England, San Francisco, Savannah Georgia, Paris France, Charleston South Carolina, Chicago, Boston, Rome Italy, Philadelphia, San Diego, Seattle, Seoul South Korea, and Atlanta!

Enjoy!

Teresa Mills

A Little About Dublin

The city of Dublin is situated on Dublin Bay at the mouth of the River Liffey. It is the capital of Ireland and its largest city. One of the more popular nicknames of Dublin is "The Fair City," which comes from a line in the city's unofficial anthem "Molly Malone":

> "In Dublin's fair city, where the girls are so pretty..."

Dublin History

Dublin is a city that has a vibrant history dating back to the 7th century with a settlement by the Gaels (a Gaelic group native to Ireland, Scotland, and the Isle of Man). Later, in the 9th century, the Vikings arrived. The Vikings, or Norsemen (Northmen) were seafaring Scandinavians (people from Denmark, Norway, or

Sweden) who left their homes looking for fortunes in other places. When the Vikings arrived in Dublin, they named their settlement "Dubh Linn" ("black pool" in Irish).

The Anglo-Norman invasion of Ireland then happened in the late 12th century. This brought more than 800 years (through 1542) of direct English (British) colonialism (taking control of another country by living there and taking advantage of it financially). The Anglo-Normans were the ruling class in England in medieval times.

In 1542, King Henry VIII of England was named King of Ireland. King Henry VIII began the British Protestant Reformation (religious reform moving through Europe in the 1500s). Ireland resisted Protestantism in favor of Catholicism for many years. In 1690, after the Jacobite war, there were two centuries of British and Protestant rule over Ireland.

In the 18th century, Dublin grew very quickly. Many Protestants immigrated to Dublin. Trade was great and Dublin became the fifth largest city in Europe.

In 1801, power shifted to London with the creation of the United Kingdom of Great Britain and Ireland.

Starting in 1845, the Great Famine (also called the Irish Potato Famine) was caused by a blight that destroyed the potato crop. This famine killed many people and caused many to leave Ireland.

In 1916 on Easter Monday, Irish Republicans rebelled against British rule. This is called the Easter Rising. The English stopped the uprising. In 1919, another rebellion against the English heavily damaged Dublin. Then in 1921, the Anglo-Irish Treaty gave Ireland the right to govern themselves. This led to internal conflicts and resulted in the Irish Civil War in 1922. After the Civil War, Northern Ireland opted out of the free state and stayed with the United Kingdom.

Dublin Today

The city of Dublin is known for several different things:

Education – It is home to several prestigious colleges and universities, including University College Dublin and Trinity College Dublin. It is a famous educational destination for international students.

A Tech Hub – Many international companies make their European headquarters in Dublin including Google, Facebook, Twitter (X), Airbnb, Microsoft, Amazon, eBay, PayPal, TikTok, and LinkedIn.

A Cultural Hub – Dublin is known for its literary heritage (home to famous writers like James Joyce, Oscar Wilde, and Samuel Beckett), theaters, and art galleries.

Tourism – There are many historic landmarks that make Dublin famous, including Trinity College, Dublin

Castle, the Guinness Storehouse, and the vibrant Temple Bar area.

Green Spaces – Dublin is home to many parks and green spaces – great places for relaxation and outdoor recreation. Phoenix Park is a great place to relax and spend the day.

We will visit many of the major landmarks and learn as much as we can about Dublin!

Are you ready?

Let's Visit Dublin!

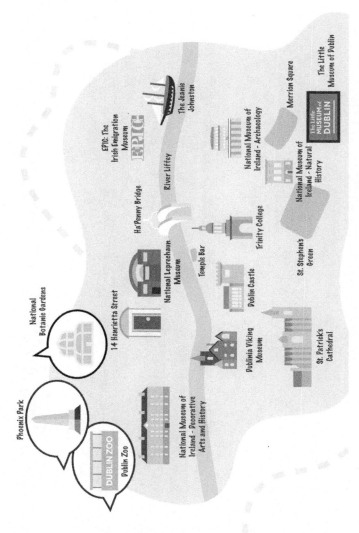

Map of Dublin Attractions

Chapter 1
Temple Bar

Temple Bar is a famous neighborhood in Dublin. It is situated along the south bank of the Liffey River. The neighborhood is home to many cultural centers including the Dublin Institute of Photography, the Irish Film Institute, the ARK (a children's cultural center), the National Photographic Archive, the Project Arts Centre, the Gaiety School of Acting, and the Irish Stock Exchange.

Temple Bar is thought to be named for Sir William Temple. Sir William built his family home in the neighborhood in the seventeenth century.

The Temple Bar

The Temple Bar

Even though the neighborhood is named Temple Bar, there is also a pub (a British name for a business that sells beer or other drinks and sometimes food) called the Temple Bar Pub. It is famous for its daily live traditional Irish music, food, and drinks. This Dublin pub has been in business since 1840.

The ARK

The ARK is an arts venue in the Temple Bar neighborhood. Its main function is to allow kids ages 2 to 12 to explore film, dance, music, literature, theater, and music. Here, kids can see performances and participate in interactive programs.

Fun Facts About The Temple Bar Area

- Temple Bar has colorful doors on many of the buildings, adding to the neighborhood's lively atmosphere.

- On weekends, the streets of Temple Bar are full of markets where you will find crafts and different foods.

- In 2011, Dave Brown set a Guinness World Record by playing the guitar for 5 days straight in the Temple Bar Pub.

Chapter 2
Trinity College

Trinity College, founded by Queen Elizabeth I in 1592, is one of the oldest colleges in the world. The college was formed when the English rule was becoming stronger in Ireland and Dublin was starting to be viewed as the capital city. The building of a university in Dublin would make the Protestant Reformation (a religious reform moving through Europe in the 1500s) stronger. The official name of the college is The College of the Holy and Undivided Trinity of Queen Elizabeth near Dublin. As of this writing, Trinity College Dublin is Ireland's top University (ranked number one in Ireland).

Trinity College Dublin Courtyard

The Library

The Library (the college's library) is the largest research library in Ireland. The library was given Legal Deposit privilege in 1801. Through this privilege, it receives copies of all materials published in Ireland and the United Kingdom. Until April of 2023, the Library was named Berkeley Library. Today it is simply called The Library.

The Library owns over 6 million printed volumes including maps, journals, and manuscripts. The most famous of the manuscripts in the library are the Book of Kells and the Book of Durrow. These were presented to the library by Henry Jones (a former vice-chancellor of the University) in the 1660s.

The Book of Kells – a manuscript written in Latin of the four Gospels of the New Testament. It is from the medieval period, crafted by Celtic monks around the year 800.

The Book of Durrow – dated to the period between 650 and 700, it is one of the oldest intact gospel books still around today.

The Old Library

This is the original library of the college. It was designed by Thomas Burgh. The Long Room in the Old Library is the main chamber. It houses more than 200,000 of the oldest books. The Old Library and Long Room are lined with marble busts of great philosophers and writers.

The Long Room is now also a venue used for meetings and events.

The Long Room in the Old Library

Fun Facts About Trinity College

- The University offers a tour called the Book of Kells Experience, a tour of the Old Library, the Long Room, exhibits about the art and collections at the library, Book of Kells 360 – a light and sound journey through the ancient masterpiece, and the Long Room re-imagined – an exhibit of the Long Room both past and present through digital reconstruction.

- Famous alumni of Trinity College Dublin include Mary Robinson (the first female President of Ireland), Oscar Wilde (an Irish playwright and poet), and Samuel Beckett (an Irish novelist and poet).

- Trinity College Dublin is known for its academic excellence. At Trinity, you can pursue a degree in engineering, arts, humanities, or sciences.

Chapter 3
Dublinia Viking Museum

Dublinia is a living history museum that brings to life the medieval Viking history of Dublin. The museum is located on the place where Dublin's Viking settlement once stood.

The museum has many interactive exhibits that lead you through busy downtown Dublin during medieval times (roughly between 1150 and 1550). Some of the things that you will see and experience in Dublinia:

- Learn what life was like on a Viking warship

- Learn about crime and punishment in early Dublin

- Learn how a toothache taken care of in earlier times

Dublinia

Fun Facts About Dublinia

- Dublinia is located in Synod Hall – part of Christ Church Cathedral.

- Dublinia is the Latin name for Dublin.

- You might meet a real Viking at Dublinia – many times there are actors roaming the museum dressed as Viking warriors.

Chapter 4
Dublin Castle

Dublin Castle was built in the 13th century and is one of the most important buildings in Irish history. The castle was the seat of English and British rule in the country of Ireland from 1204 until 1922.

When the castle was built, it was built as a medieval fortress (a strong or well-protected place that would be hard for enemies to enter) by orders of King John of England. It has four corner towers that were linked by tall curtain walls (defense walls between fortified towers) creating an enclosed area.

In 1684 a fire caused quite a bit of damage to the castle, but parts of the medieval structure remain today.

Dublin Castle Record Tower - built around 1228

There are daily guided tours of the castle including:

The Viking Excavation Site – a tour under the castle reveals some of the original medieval castle construction and some of the original defenses of the castle. You will see steps leading down to the moat (a deep trench around a fort or castle usually filled with water).

The Chapel Royal – a beautiful chapel designed by Francis Johnston. This chapel opened in 1814 and was named the Anglican Chapel of the Viceroy. After King George IV attended services in 1821, the chapel was referred to as Chapel Royal. Although this chapel has been around since 1814, the first chapel at the castle was opened around 1242.

The State Apartments – the State Apartments were both residential and public quarters for the viceregal court (a group of people who have the job of representing a king or queen). Today the apartments host Ireland's presidential inaugurations and other prestigious functions.

Fun Facts About Dublin Castle

- The site of the castle was originally a Viking settlement.
- St. Patrick's Hall is the grandest and largest room in the State Apartments.
- A hidden treasure on the castle grounds is the Dubh Linn Gardens.

Chapter 5
National Museum of Ireland

The National Museum of Ireland is a state-run (controlled by the government) museum system. It was created by an act of Parliament in 1877 called the Science and Art Museum Act of 1877. The first name of the museum was The Museum of Science and Art. Leading up to the Science and Art Museum Act of 1877, buildings and collections were transferred to the state (the government) by the RDS (Royal Dublin Society), the RIA (Royal Irish Academy), and Trinity College.

The museum system has four different museums at this time:

The National Museum of Ireland – Archaeology (Dublin)

Located on Kildare Street, this museum opened its doors in 1890. It went through several different names before finally becoming The National Museum of Ireland – Archaeology in 1921. Some of the fascinating things to see at this museum include:

- **The Ardagh Chalice** – a work of Celtic art, this medieval artwork chalice dates back to the 8th century.

- **The Tara Brooch** – the brooch (an ornamental piece of jewelry that attaches to clothing with a hinged pin) is made from bronze, gold, and silver and dates back to the 7th-8th century.

The National Museum of Ireland - Decorative Arts & History (Dublin)

This museum is located in the old Collins Barracks, a former military barracks. In this museum, you will find military history collections, jewelry, coins, furniture, and clothing. Some of the cool things to see at this museum are:

- **The Fonthill Vase** – this vase is documented as the earliest piece of porcelain to come from China to Europe. The vase was made between 1300 and 1340 AD.

- **Soldiers & Chiefs Exhibit** – follow the history of Ireland's military from 1550 through the 21st century.

- **The Asgard** – a yacht that was built in 1905 by Norwegian naval architect Colin Archer.

The National Museum of Ireland - Decorative Arts & History

The National Museum of Ireland - Natural History (Dublin)

Also known as the "Dead Zoo," this museum was built in 1856. This museum has more than 10,000 exhibits of birds, fish, insects, and mammals from around the world! Some of the best things to see at this museum:

- **Giant Irish Deer** – skeletons of the giant Irish deer have large antler spans – up to 3.5 meters (11.5 feet).

- **Irish Wildlife** – there is a display of a badger family, otters, and pine martens that have been expertly taxidermized (an animal stuffed or mounted for display).

- **The Wonder Cabinet** – an interactive zone in the museum that allows kids and adults to get up close and touch bones and fossils.

The National Museum of Ireland – Country Life (Castlebar, County Mayo)

This museum is located 225 km (140 miles) northwest of Dublin. It is dedicated to Ireland's rural past. Some of the exhibits to see are:

- **The Times: Rural Ireland, 1850-1950** – a timeline of important historical events that affected rural Ireland.

- **Cycling the Country** – bicycles were an important mode of transportation in Ireland from the 1930s forward. This exhibit gives a history of bicycles and bicycling in rural Ireland.

- **Straw, Hay, and Rushes** – this exhibit celebrates the smart people who could make money by making something from raw materials. They made things such as straw dresses, baskets, mats and mattresses, beehives, chairs, etc., just about anything you can think of.

HEY KIDS! LET'S VISIT DUBLIN IRELAND

The National Museum of Ireland – Country Life

Fun Facts About The National Museum of Ireland

- Admission to the National Museum of Ireland is free!

- The National Museum of Ireland – Archaeology has one of the best collections of Viking pieces anywhere.

- At The National Museum of Ireland – Country Life, you can learn all about fun, traditional games that were played in rural Ireland and play these games yourself.

Chapter 6
St Stephen's Green

St Stephen's Green is a public park and garden space in the city center of Dublin. The park is a 9-hectare (22-acre) rectangle. The park has been maintained with the same Victorian layout as the original design.

The park's name comes from St Stephen's Church which was in this same area in the 13th century. The park's land was a marshy area that the citizens used for grazing livestock. This continued until 1663 when the city decided to use the ground for a park. The park was created with an area next to it used as building lots. The rent generated through the building lots was used to build walls and pave roads in the park.

St Stephen's Green

Throughout the 17th century, the park flourished as a very fashionable place. There was a walkway in the park at that time called the Beaux Walk, which was a very popular place for high society people to walk in their fine clothing. It was a scene of elegance and taste.

During the 19th century, the park deteriorated badly. In 1814, control of the park fell to the local homeowners through a commission. They did some cleaning up and replaced the broken walls and damaged walkways. These improvements led to the park being closed to the public and only accessible to any who would pay the commission. This caused hard feelings between the public and the commission.

In 1877, Sir Arthur Guinness (of the Guinness brewing family) offered to buy the Green from the commission.

He would then return the park to the public. He paid the park's debts and made sure that the park was run by the Commission of Public Works. Sir Arthur Guinness then had the park landscaped and redeveloped. This took three years, and the newly redesigned park was opened on July 27, 1880.

Fun Facts About St Stephen's Green

- St Stephen's Green was used as a place of public executions and witch burnings before 1663.

- The park has approximately 750 trees and shrubs along with many flowers!

- Among the many statues in the park are statues of Arthur Guinness and James Joyce (famous author and poet from Dublin).

Chapter 7

Little Museum of Dublin

This small award-winning ("Dublin's best museum experience" ~Irish Times, and "Certificate of Excellence" ~TripAdvisor) museum set in an 18th-century Georgian townhouse is one of Dublin's most charming museums. The museum opened for business in 2011 after asking the public for historic objects. The response for items for the museum was huge, and today there are more than 5,000 items in the collection. This collection is housed on the museum's first floor as a permanent collection.

The Little Museum of Dublin offers its **Famous Guided Tour** — an hour-long tour that is both classic and entertaining. It is a walk-through that starts in 1900s Dublin and then moves on to more modern history. A room on the second floor of the museum is dedicated to the history of U2, a famous rock band from Dublin.

In addition to the tour of the museum, you can take part in **The Big Little Treasure Hunt** – a treasure hunt through St. Stephen's Green. It is a fun way to learn some Irish history.

The I Love Dublin Children's program is a free class offered to all schoolchildren in Ireland. The program teaches about Dublin's heritage.

Fun Facts About the Little Museum of Dublin

- Inside the museum is the lectern that was used by United States President John F. Kennedy when he visited Ireland in 1963.

- One exhibit in the museum is a recreation of the Irish Times from 1934 to 1954 when Robert "Bertie" Smyllie was editor. Smyllie's desk and typewriter are in the editor's room exhibit.

- The tour guides are one of the main attractions at the museum. These guides fill the museum with song and laughter.

Chapter 8
Saint Patrick's Cathedral

Saint Patrick's Cathedral is one of the most visited places in Dublin. The present cathedral building was built between 1220 and 1260 and is one of the few buildings remaining from Dublin's medieval times. The present church building is constructed of local limestone and stone imported from Bristol, England.

The church was built to honor one of the patron saints of Ireland, Saint Patrick. It is built on the site of a well that is believed to have been used by Saint Patrick himself. Saint Patrick is credited with bringing Christianity to Ireland and used the three-leafed shamrock to explain the Holy Trinity (God the Father, Jesus the Son, and the Holy Spirit) while preaching.

Saint Patrick's Cathedral

Saint Patrick's Cathedral is open for tours daily and services are held at the church regularly.

Fun Facts About Saint Patrick and Saint Patrick's Cathedral

- Jonathan Swift, author of *Gulliver's Travels*, is buried on the Saint Patrick's Cathedral grounds.

- St. Patrick's Day is celebrated on the day that Saint Patrick passed away (March 17). Even though we celebrate by wearing green on that day, Saint Patrick normally wore blue robes.

- Some sort of church has existed on this site for more than 1000 years. The first church, probably a wooden one, was built around 1191.

Chapter 9
Merrion Square

Merrion Square is one of Dublin's largest and grandest public park squares. The park is lined on three sides with Georgian Houses (houses normally built between 1714 and 1830 with symmetrical windows, columns, and shutters). The houses are now mainly used as office spaces but have plaques detailing any rich and famous person who once lived there. Some examples of previous residents are William Butler Yeats (Irish poet and writer), Daniel O'Connell (former Lord mayor of Dublin), and Oscar Wilde (Irish poet and playwright).

The park is a respite featuring colorful flowers and shrubs. On Sundays, you will find artists hanging their works around the square for sale. Look for the statue of Oscar Wilde in the park!

Colorful Doors on Georgian Houses around Merrion Square

Oscar Wilde Statue in Merrion Square

Fun Facts About Merrion Square

- Merrion Square Park was once a private park with only residents having keys to enter. In the 1970s, the park opened to the public.

- The park's land used to belong to the Roman Catholic Church and was almost used as the site of a Roman Catholic cathedral. The cathedral would have complemented the Church of Ireland's St Patrick's Cathedral and Christ Church. They eventually decided to build on Marlborough St instead.

- In Georgian Dublin, many of the Merrion Square homes would hold salons (a private social gathering where guests would discuss politics, philosophy, literature, or art) in their homes. People would leave their country estates for these social gatherings.

Chapter 10
Dublin Mountains

The Dublin Mountains are part of the Wicklow Mountains that are in County Dublin. The mountains and the trails are a short drive south from the city of Dublin and can make for a great escape from the city. The Dublin Mountains offer many walking and hiking experiences in the 43 km (27 miles) of trails, paths, and roads.

View of Dublin from Fairy Castle in Dublin Mountains

Road approaching the Dublin Mountains

Fun Facts About the Dublin Mountains

- The Dublin Mountains form a natural border between County Dublin and County Wicklow.

- The highest peak in the Dublin Mountains is Kippure Mountain at 757 m (2,484 feet) in elevation.

- You can see beautiful views over Dublin with hikes on easy to moderate rolling hills – a great way to escape the city!

- Fairy Castle Loop is a hiking trail in the Dublin Mountains. One of the photos in this chapter was taken from this trail.

Chapter 11
Ha'Penny Bridge

Officially called the Liffey Bridge, the Ha'Penny Bridge is a pedestrian (for walkers, not cars) bridge that crosses the River Liffey. It was built in 1816 and is made of cast iron. The Ha'Penny Bridge is one of three pedestrian bridges in use in Dublin today, but it was the only one until the Millennium Bridge was built in 1999. The third pedestrian bridge is the Sean O'Casey Bridge which was built in 2005.

This bridge is 43 m (141 feet) long and 3.6 m (12 feet) wide. The cast iron bridge was forged in Shropshire, England, and was transported to Dublin via ship. The bridge was then assembled on-site and opened for foot traffic on May 19, 1816.

At the time it was built, there were seven ferries that transported people across the River Liffey. The ferries, owned by William Walsh, were in need of repair. So, when the new bridge was constructed, it was leased to

Walsh to manage. Instead of charging for ferry service, he was given the right to charge a ha'penny (half a penny) for anyone who crossed the bridge for the next 100 years.

The Ha'Penny Bridge

Fun Facts About the Ha'Penny Bridge

- This is Dublin's oldest pedestrian bridge and is still in use today with close to 30,000 people crossing it every day.

- Approximately 85% of the ironwork on the bridge today is the original metal.

- The name of the bridge was originally planned to be the Wellington Bridge, for the Dublin-born Duke of Wellington as a celebration of his defeat of Napoleon at Waterloo. The name never stuck with Dubliners.

Chapter 12

The Jeanie Johnston - Irish Famine Story

A big part of the history of Ireland is the Great Famine (also called the Irish Potato Famine) lasting from 1845 to 1852. This time was a period of disease and famine (when many people could not get enough food for an extended period of time). The Great Famine had a major impact on the country of Ireland with the loss of almost 1/4 of its population from death or fleeing the country.

One of the main contributing causes of the Great Famine was an infection of the potato crops by blight (a disease that makes plants wither and die), causing the potatoes to rot. Prior to the famine, Ireland was dependent on the potato and planted a lot of them. Potatoes were easy to plant and fed a lot of people. The disease that affected the potatoes crippled Ireland. On top of that, government policies in place at the time made access to other food sources very difficult.

That's where the Jeanie Johnston comes into the story. The Jeanie Johnston was one of the "famine ships" that was used to help people leave Ireland during the famine. Between 1848 and 1855, there were 16 voyages aboard the Jeanie Johnston taking passengers to North America.

The Replica Jeanie Johnston in Dublin Docklands

The Jeanie Johnston carried up to 248 passengers on the 47-day (average transit time) transatlantic voyage to Quebec, Baltimore, or New York. This is amazing as the replica of the Jeanie Johnston in the Dublin Harbor is only licensed to carry 40 people total (crew and passengers).

The replica Jeanie Johnston is open to the public for tours. The tour (which lasts approximately 50 minutes) allows visitors to tour the ship and learn about the trip to North America and how the passengers spent their days.

Facts About the Jeanie Johnston

- Despite the conditions and the number of people aboard the Jeanie Johnston at one time, no passenger or crew lost their lives onboard the ship.

- The Jeanie Johnston had the reputation of looking after its passengers, unlike other ships that transported famine refugees. The Jeanie Johnston had a medical doctor aboard and the ship was not overly crowded.

- Space on the ship was tight, but each passenger was provided a daily food ration and allowed time on the deck for fresh air each day.

Chapter 13
EPIC Irish Emigration Museum

Another large part of Irish history is its history of emigration (leaving one's home country to settle in another) and diaspora (spread of people from their home country). It is so much a part of Ireland that Dublin has a museum dedicated to people who have left Ireland, why they left, and how those who left influenced the world.

Statistics show that more than 70 million people worldwide have Irish roots. That's from a country with a population of just over 5 million. So, the story of Ireland is really not complete without the stories of those who left the country.

One major reason for emigration from Ireland was the Great Famine in the 1800s. Ireland is the only country in Europe to have a lower population at the end of the 19th century than at the beginning.

The EPIC Museum tells the stories of the over 10 million people who have left Ireland. You will learn some of the reasons that they left, where they went, and how they influenced the world later. The museum is laid out in 20 different interactive galleries that help tell the stories. The museum recommends allowing 90 minutes to complete the self-guided tour and then spend longer looking around!

Arial view of the EPIC Irish Emigration Museum

Some of the emigration stories that you will learn about in the museum include:

- Cedric Gibbons – Oscar (US based Academy of Motion Picture Arts and Sciences award) statue designer.

- James Hoban – designer of the White House (Washington DC).

- The twenty-three US presidents who claim Irish Ancestry, including Joe Biden, James Buchanan, George H. W. Bush, George W. Bush, and John F. Kennedy.

If you have Irish ancestry, you can visit the Irish Family History Center (IFHC) at the museum. The IFHC has a resident genealogy expert and records that might be able to help you discover more about your own past.

Fun Facts About Irish Emigration and the EPIC Museum

- EPIC stands for Every Person Is Connected.

- The EPIC museum opened in 2016 and was described by the Irish Times as "the world's first fully digital museum." It had more than 120,000 visitors in its first year of operation.

- Since 1820, it is estimated that more than 6 million people have emigrated from Ireland to the United States.

Chapter 14
National Leprechaun Museum

The National Leprechaun Museum is a first of its kind. It is a museum dedicated to the folklore Irish myth – the leprechaun. The guided tour through the museum takes less than an hour and explores what it would be like to live as a leprechaun and follow them to the end of a rainbow in search of gold.

The museum explains the legendary leprechaun through storytelling traditions. The storytellers focus on traditional Irish tales and bring the leprechauns into their stories. You can actually think of the museum as a storytelling museum.

Playful Cartoon Leprechaun

Fun Facts About Leprechauns

- Leprechauns are usually drawn as mischievous (playfully causing trouble) bearded men wearing a coat and hat.

- Irish folklore depicts leprechauns as smallish men who guard hidden treasure like pots of gold.

- Other stories of leprechauns depict them as loners who enjoy practical jokes (tricks played on someone to make fun of them).

What would you do if you ran into a leprechaun?

Chapter 15

National Botanic Gardens

The National Botanic Gardens of Ireland are located about 5 km (3.2 miles) northwest of the city of Dublin. The gardens are 19.5 hectares (48 acres) and were founded in 1795 by the Dublin Society, which later became the Royal Dublin Society. Between this location close to Dublin and the satellite location in County Wicklow, there are approximately 20,000 living plants. Botanic Gardens admission is free.

The glasshouses in the gardens are very nicely planted and maintained. These glasshouses are the centerpiece of the botanical gardens. The glasshouses are formed from a freestanding cast and wrought iron frame with windows in the frame. The Curvilinear Range and the Great Palm House glasshouses are considered some of the finest in Europe in terms of artistic merit and technical innovation.

National Botanic Garden Great Palm Glasshouse (side view)

Curvilinear Range Glasshouse

The botanical gardens are very involved in conservation (maintenance of natural resources). Because of this, the gardens are home to over 300 endangered plant species from all over the world. The plants are studied and carefully cared for there.

Fun Facts About the National Botanic Gardens

- The Botanic Gardens was the first place that the potato blight was identified at the start of the Irish Potato Famine. Research was carried out at the gardens throughout the famine to help stop the infection.

- An Austrian philosopher, Ludwig Wittgenstein, spent time in Ireland during the winter of 1948-49. During that time, he spent much time at the Palm glasshouse writing. There is a plaque at the steps where he sat to commemorate this.

- There is a college of horticulture (the art and science of growing plants, flowers, fruits, or vegetables), the Teagasc College of Amenity Horticulture, located in the gardens. Amenity horticulture covers both gardening and landscaping.

Chapter 16
14 Henrietta Street

14 Henrietta Street is a museum in Dublin that is also referred to as the Tenement Museum. It has been open since 2018 and is one of Ireland's famous tenement houses. A tenement house is a house that is divided and rented as separate residences, usually a run-down house.

The home at 14 Henrietta Street was built in the late 1740s as a single-family home. It was owned by Lord Viscount Molesworth and his wife Mary Jenney Usher. Throughout the 18th century, the home had other wealthy residents. In 1801, with the uniting of Great Britain (England and Scotland) and Ireland, Dublin lost governmental status. This caused many leading officials to return to London. So, beginning in the 19th century, 14 Henrietta Street was a home to professionals such as lawyers.

During the Irish Potato Famine, more and more people from rural Ireland moved into the city, causing overcrowding. In 1876, 14 Henrietta Street was purchased by Thomas Vance and turned into a tenement house with 14 separate apartments. During this time, 835 people lived in the 15 homes along Henrietta Street (that includes the 14 apartments at 14 Henrietta Street). The living conditions were very bad in these tenement homes. Amazingly, people lived like this up until 1979 when the last resident of this home left.

Representative Tenement Home in Dublin

Fun Facts About 14 Henrietta Street

- A tour of 14 Henrietta Street connects stories of the home's residents over 300 years, from its grand Georgian beginnings to its time as a tenement slum house.

- Former residents of 14 Henrietta Street have been heavily involved in creating some of the exhibits that are in the museum.

- By the late 1990s, the home had decayed and rotted. The City stepped in and renovated the home. It was restored in three different phases over 10 years at a cost of nearly 5 million euros (5.5 million dollars).

Chapter 17
Phoenix Park

Phoenix Park is a completely enclosed park, and it is the largest public enclosed park in any European capital city. The 707-hectare (1,750-acre) park is completely enclosed by an 11-km (6.8-mile) perimeter wall. The park was originally designed to be a royal hunting park in the 1660s. It was opened to the public in 1747.

Some of the fascinating structures that you will see in Phoenix Park include:

Wellington Tower – a 62 m (203 foot) tall obelisk (like the Washington Monument in Washington DC) built in 1861 to commemorate the victories of the Duke of Wellington including the Battle of Waterloo.

Phoenix Column – a column crafted from Portland stone (stone from the Isle of Portland in Dorset, England) in 1747.

Papal Cross – this marks the spot where Pope John Paul II preached in 1979. Later, Pope Francis celebrated mass at the Papal Cross in 2018.

Dublin Zoo – Phoenix Park is home to the Dublin Zoo.

Phoenix Park

Fun Facts About Phoenix Park

- There are close to 40 Vikings buried in the largest Viking cemetery outside of Scandinavia, which is located in Phoenix Park.

- Winston Churchill, former British Prime Minister, lived in the Viceregal Lodge in Phoenix Park between the ages of 2 and 6. Churchill's father was the personal secretary to the Viceroy at this time.

- Phoenix Park was actually started as a deer park. The fallow deer still roam the park grounds today. A fallow deer is an elegant mid-sized deer with a spotted coat.

- The park is the home (official residence) of the President of Ireland as well as the U.S. Ambassador.

Chapter 18
Dublin Zoo

The Dublin Zoo is located in Phoenix Park. The zoo covers over 28 hectares (69 acres) and is home to hundreds of animals. The zoo opened privately in 1831 and to the public in 1840. Today, the Dublin Zoo sees over 1 million visitors per year.

Some of the habitats you might see at the Dublin Zoo are:

The African Savanna – home to giraffes, white rhinos, zebras, and ostriches.

Giraffes at the Dublin Zoo

The Himalayan Hills – a Himalayan mountain range is home to snow leopards and red pandas.

Wolves in the Woods – grey wolves in their natural environment of woodlands.

Kaziranga Forest Trail – the home of Dublin Zoo's elephants.

The South American House – home to more than nine different species of monkeys all finding their own place in the forest.

Zoorasic World – home of the reptiles of the zoo. Here you will see crocodiles, pythons, rat snakes, and more.

The Nocturnal House – home to the creatures of the night, the aye-ayes (a nocturnal lemur species).

HEY KIDS! LET'S VISIT DUBLIN IRELAND

Gorilla Rainforest – home to a group of western lowland gorillas.

The Orangutan Forest – a habitat that offers climbing adventures for orangutans.

An orangutan in the Dublin Zoo

Sea Lion Cove – home to a colony of California sea lions.

Fun Facts About the Dublin Zoo

- Ice skating on the lake in the zoo is not allowed and has not been allowed since before 1860. But when harsh winters hit in the 1860s, the lake appeared to be frozen so several people decided to ice skate on it. The ice cracked and 21 people had to be rescued.

- The Dublin Zoo has been featured in a TV series called "The Zoo," which can now be seen on Apple TV. The show became a fan favorite in Ireland.

- When the zoo opened in 1840, the entrance price was only one penny on Sundays. The entrance on other days in 1840 was six pence (6 pennies).

Chapter 19
Dún Laoghaire Harbor

In the late 17th century and early 18th century, Dublin Harbor had problems with shifting sandbars and silt that caused some ships to have to dock farther out and tender passengers (move passengers to a smaller boat to transfer them from the ship) to shore if the tides or weather would not allow docking. The problems at the Dublin port caused inconvenience and frequent shipwrecks with no protection from storms.

The frequent problems with the harbor came to a head in 1807 when two ships (the Prince of Wales and the Rochdale) left from Dublin and were driven into rocks along the coast close to Blackrock (slightly south of Dublin) and resulted in the loss of more than 400 lives.

A search began for a place to locate an asylum harbor (a harbor that would provide shelter from a storm) with the

Dublin Harbor Act of 1816. This act allowed the building of a major port to serve Dublin that would also be a safe port for ships during storms.

Following the legislation, the seaside town of Dún Laoghaire was found to be a suitable location for such a harbor. The town and Dún Laoghaire Harbor are approximately 12 km (7.5 miles) from Dublin. Dún Laoghaire was originally called Dunleary or Dun Lerroy. In 1820, after King George IV sailed from the port, it was called Kingstown for more than 100 years.

By 1834, the harbor had helped to shelter more than 3,000 boats even though it was only partially completed. Harbor construction continued, and now it includes an east pier and a west pier that almost completely enclose the harbor. Each pier has a lighthouse. The East Pier lighthouse was completed in 1842 and further enhanced with the Carlisle Pier, a ferry terminal in 1856. The West Pier Lighthouse was also completed in the mid-1850s. The railroad was connected in 1856 and a railway station opened in 1859. In 1920, the name became Dún Laoghaire and in 1924 the Harbor was officially named Dún Laoghaire Harbor.

View of the East Pier and West Pier Lighthouses

Fun Facts About Dún Laoghaire Harbor

- Construction on the harbor began in 1817 but was not complete until 1859 – 42 years!

- Queen Victoria made a special visit to the harbor in 1900. A very expensive wooden pier was built for her.

- The Carlisle Pier in the Dún Laoghaire Harbor has been named the Pier of Tears because of the number of emigrants from the country from this harbor.

Chapter 20
Dublin Tours

Dublin is such a friendly and interesting city. It is full of history! One of the best ways to get an overview of the city and hear some history is to take a tour. Here are some options for tours.

Walking Tour with Locals

This is a great idea for learning as much as you can in Dublin. The local tour guide takes a small group around town for a tour. This gives you a lot of time to ask questions and get suggestions for other things to do and see.

Viking Splash

The Viking Splash tour is a great option for families. This tour is aboard a WW2 (World War II) amphibious DUKWs (a six-wheel truck used by the US military during World War II. D – model year 1942, U – body

Style U amphibious, K – all-wheel drive, W – dual rear axles). The DUKW is called a "duck."

The tour is on land and in the water.

Hop On, Hop Off Bus Tours

The hop on, hop off buses are always a great way to see the city and get a nice idea of where things are! Check out these buses in the city center and grab one for a round-trip tour of the city. Get an overview of the history of Dublin, decide all that you want to see, and then go exploring further!

I hope you enjoyed your trip to Dublin! I have a fun puzzle and coloring page download to go along with the book. This fun addition is free to download here:

kid-friendly-family-vacations.com/dublinfun

Please consider adding a review to help other readers learn more about Dublin whether traveling or learning from home. Thanks!

kid-friendly-family-vacations.com/review-dublin

Also By Teresa Mills and Kid Friendly Family Vacations

Hey Kids! Let's Visit Washington DC
Hey Kids! Let's Visit A Cruise Ship
Hey Kids! Let's Visit New York City
Hey Kids! Let's Visit London England
Hey Kids! Let's Visit San Francisco
Hey Kids! Let's Visit Savannah Georgia
Hey Kids! Let's Visit Paris France
Hey Kids! Let's Visit Charleston South Carolina
Hey Kids! Let's Visit Chicago
Hey Kids! Let's Visit Rome Italy
Hey Kids! Let's Visit Boston
Hey Kids! Let's Visit Philadelphia
Hey Kids! Let's Visit San Diego
Hey Kids! Let's Visit Seattle
Hey Kids! Let's Visit Seoul South Korea
Hey Kids! Let's Visit Atlanta
Hey Kids! Let's Visit Dublin Ireland

More from Kid Friendly Family Vacations

BOOKS

Books to help build your kids / grandkids life experiences through travel and learning
https://kid-friendly-family-vacations.com/books

COLORING AND ACTIVITY PAGKAGES

Coloring pages, activity books, printable travel journals, and more in our Etsy shop
https://kid-friendly-family-vacations.com/etsy

RESOURCES FOR TEACHERS

Resources for teachers on Teachers Pay Teachers
https://kid-friendly-family-vacations.com/tpt

It is our mission to help you build your children's and grand-children's life experiences through travel. Not just traveling with your kids... building their Life Experiences"! Join our community here:
https://kid-friendly-family-vacations.com/join

Attributions

Editing and Proofreading

Katie Erickson – katieericksonediting.com

Cover Photos

Trinity College - Courtyard- © jbyard / depositphotos.com

Dublin Castle – © byggarn79 / depositphotos.com

Ha'Penny Bridge - © vmacphoto /sdepositphotos.com

The Jeanie Johnston - © Dudlajzov / depositphotos.com

Dublin Zoo - orangutan - © igabriela / depositphotos.com

Photos in Book

Temple Bar - © icenando / depositphotos.com

Trinity College - Courtyard- © jbyard / depositphotos.com

Trinity College – Long Room – © icarmen13 / depositphotos.com

Dublinia and Christ Church Cathedral- © Dudlajzov / depositphotos.com

Dublin Castle – © byggarn79 / depositphotos.com

National Museum of Ireland - Decorative Arts and History - © Dudlajzov / depositphotos.com

National Museum of Ireland - Country Life - © Frank Bach / shutterstock.com

St Stephens Green - © Dudlajzov / depositphotos.com

St Patrick's Cathedral - © tatulaju / depositphotos.com

Merrion Square - © RudiErnst / depositphotos.com

Merrion Square - Oscar Wilde statue - © Wirestock / depositphotos.com

Dublin Mountains - © rafalstachura / depositphotos.com

Dublin Mountains - view of Dublin from Fairy Castle - © romanoverko / depositphotos.com

Ha'Penny Bridge - © vmacphoto /sdepositphotos.com

The Jeanie Johnston - © Dudlajzov / depositphotos.com

EPIC The Irish Emigration Museum - © Alexey Fedorenko / shutterstock.com

Leprechan - © Dazdraperma / depositphotos.com

National Botanic Gardens - © BarkKowski / depositphotos.com

National Botanic Gardens - Curvilinear Range- © jordache / depositphotos.com

14 Henrietta Street - Tenement House - © Derick P. Hudson / shutterstock.com

Phoenix Park - © Dudlajzov / depositphotos.com

Dublin Zoo - giraffes - © DawidKalisinski / depositphotos.com

Dublin Zoo - orangutan - © igabriela / depositphotos.com

Dún Laoghaire - © romanoverko / depositphotos.com

About the Author

Teresa Mills is the bestselling author of the "Hey Kids! Let's Visit..." Book Series for Kids! Teresa's goal through her books and website is to help parents / grandparents who want to build the life experiences of their children / grandchildren through travel and learning activities.

She is an active mother and Mimi. She and her family love traveling in the USA, and internationally too! They love exploring new places, eating cool foods, and having yet another adventure as a family! With the Mills, it's all about traveling as family.

In addition to traveling, Teresa enjoys reading, hiking, biking, and helping others.

Join in the fun at

kid-friendly-family-vacations.com

Made in United States
Orlando, FL
08 June 2024

47634076R00055